I Like Being ♡ ME ♡

*Poems for Children
About Feeling Special,
Appreciating Others,
and Getting Along*

Written by
Judy Lalli

Photographs by
Douglas L. Mason-Fry

free spirit
PUBLiSHiNG®
Works
for kids™

Copyright © 1997 by Judy Lalli

Library of Congress Cataloging-in-Publication Data

Lalli, Judy, 1949–
    I like being me : poems for children about feeling special, appreciating others, and getting along / written by Judy Lalli ; photographs by Douglas L. Mason-Fry.
        p.   cm.
    Summary: A collection of poems about being kind, solving problems, learning from mistakes, telling the truth, dealing with feelings, being a friend, and more.
    ISBN 1-57542-025-2
    1. Interpersonal relations--Juvenile poetry.   2. Self-esteem--Juvenile poetry.   3. Children's poetry, American.   [1. Identity--Poetry.   2. Self-esteem--Poetry.   3. American poetry.]
    I. Mason-Fry, Douglas L., 1950- ill.   II. Title.
    PS3562.A412I18   1997
    811'.54--dc21   97-11653
                                            CIP
                                            AC

Edited by Marjorie Lisovskis
Cover design by Ann Elliot Artz
Interior design by Julie Smith and Robin Stearns
Author photograph by John Kellar Photography

10 9 8 7 6 5 4 3 2
Printed in Canada

Free Spirit Publishing Inc.
400 First Avenue North, Suite 616
Minneapolis, Minnesota 55401-1730
(612) 338-2068
help4kids@freespirit.com

Dedication

To Diane, for enthusiastically field testing the poems
    with her students
To Doug, for taking pictures that bring wonder to my words
To Jim, for encouraging me to persevere with the idea for
    this book
To Mary Martha, for giving honest and caring feedback that
    enriched the project
And to Tony, for giving technical support on the computer
    and unconditional support to me.

Acknowledgments

The beautiful children whose photographs appear on these pages include students from Paul V. Fly School in Norristown, Pennsylvania, where I teach. There is also an appearance by the photographer's son.

I am especially grateful to the students in my class, who were my first editors. They would eagerly await the arrival of the new poems, "hot off the computer." We would read them, recite them, and discuss them. If the words didn't flow, or if the rhythms seemed forced, I knew that I had to make changes, some of which the children suggested. And when I was afraid that children wouldn't "get" the point of a poem, my students frequently reassured me and, in doing so, reminded me of how much children really are capable of understanding. As the first poem in the book asserts, they can all be winners. I appreciate learning that lesson from them.

Contents

Dear Reader,

I think poems are fun. You can read them quietly to yourself or aloud to others. You can think about what they mean or just enjoy the sounds of the words. You can recite favorite poems over and over until they're a part of you and you know them by heart.

Photographs are fun, too. They can bring special meanings to words or give you new ideas. You can think about what's happening in a picture and wonder what might happen next. You can pretend that you're in a picture and imagine how you would feel.

I hope you enjoy the poems and photographs in this book. And I hope you like being you!

Love,

Judy Lalli

I Can Choose

I can choose
To win or lose.
I know it's up to me.

If I think that
I'm a winner,
That's what I will be!

I'm Waiting for a Rainbow

I'm waiting for a rainbow,
I'm waiting for the sun.
I'm waiting for the rain to stop
So I can play and run.

I know I should be patient,
But waiting's such a pain.
I guess I'll have to pass the time
Appreciating rain.

I Hear the Music Playing

I hear the music playing,
But I don't remember the song.

I hear the teacher talking,
But I get the directions wrong.

I hear the children reading,
But I miss where to follow along.

My hearing seems to be okay,
But my listening isn't strong.

I Didn't Believe I Could Do It

I didn't believe I could do it.
I was afraid to try.
My *teacher* believed I could do it,
And next time, so will I.

Mistakes Can Be Good

Mistakes can be good.
They can help you grow.
They can show you what you need to know.

So whenever you make a mistake,
Just say:
"Now I'll try another way."

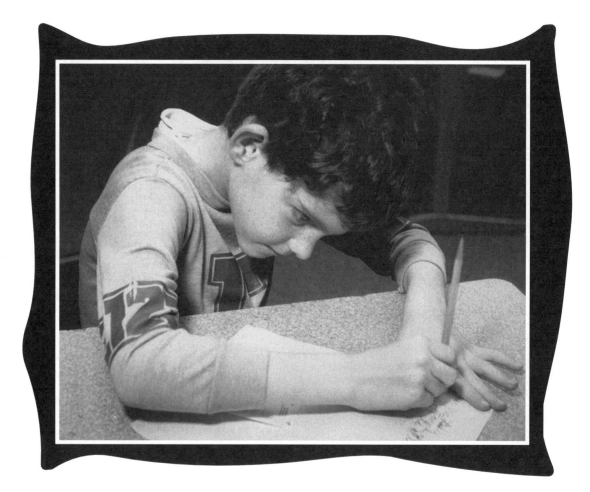

At Least I'm Getting Better

I run and run and run and run,
And then I trip and fall.
I throw and catch and throw and catch,
And then I drop the ball.

I write my name and write my name,
And then I miss a letter.
But everybody makes mistakes.
At least I'm getting better!

Who Should I Be?

Who should I be on dress-up day?
I can wear a mask—
It's fun to play.

I can't decide who I should be,
Because most of the time
I like being me!

Broken Wagon

I'm mad.
It looks bad.
I think I broke my wagon.

It has a dent.
The wheel is bent.
And everything is draggin'.

The handle's loose.
Oh, what's the use?
I hope somebody kicks it.

I want to shout
And throw it out!
But I think I'd better fix it.

If I Promise to Do It

If I promise to do it,
I'll do it.

If I promise to go,
I'll be there.

If I promise to finish,
I'll finish.

Keeping my word
Shows I care.

Grandma Says

Grandma says I shouldn't lie,
The truth is always better.
I just hope she doesn't ask
If I like my birthday sweater.

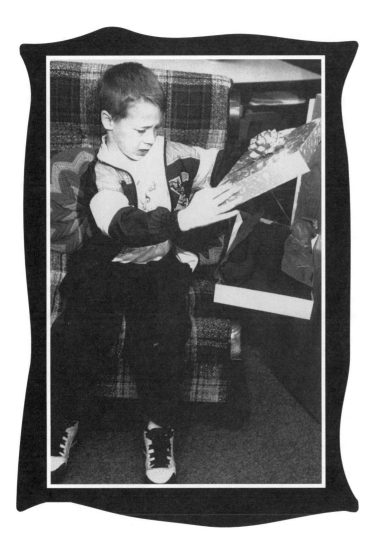

Don't Say "Crybaby!"

Don't say "Crybaby!"
Don't say "Dummy!"
Teasing makes me
Feel so crummy.

Falling down
Can bruise my knees,
But words can hurt
Where no one sees.

24

When I'm Cranky

When I'm cranky
I sass my mother,
I stamp my feet,
I boss my brother.

I think what I should do instead
Is jog,
Or jump,
Or go to bed.

I'm a Person, Too

I'm not as big as you,
But I'm a person, too.
So treat me with respect,
And that's how I'll treat you.

Someone Else's Chair

Want to learn about each other?
Want to show how much you care?
Just imagine what it's like
To sit in someone else's chair.

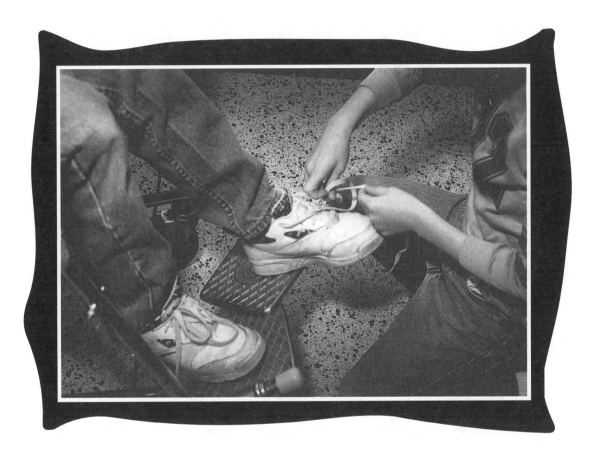

I Don't Have the Time

I don't have the time.
I don't really care.

I don't want to do it.
I don't think it's fair.

I don't want to help you.
Can't you understand?

WHOOPS! I slipped!
Will you give me a hand?

I Can't Move It

I can't move it,
You can't move it,
It won't move an inch.

But if we work together,
Moving it's a cinch.

Hands

Hands can fight,
Hands can scare,
Or hands can join together
To show they care.

Someone Who Knows How to Share

If one of us needs an eraser,
An eraser will be there,
Because it's fun
To be someone
Who knows how to share.

If one of us loses a pencil,
Another one will be there,
Because it's fun
To be someone
Who knows how to share.

And whenever we do something special,
We do it as a pair,
Because it's fun
To be someone
Who knows how to share.

I Hope You're As Lucky As I Am

I hope you have someone to play with,
Someone who cares what you say.
I hope you are always together—
Even if one goes away.

I hope you can share all your feelings,
I hope you don't have to pretend.
I hope you're as lucky as I am—
I hope someone calls you a friend.

Five Little People

Five little people went out to play.

The first one said, "Do it my way!"
The second one said, "That's not fair!"
The third one said, "I don't care!"
The fourth one said, "This isn't fun!"
The fifth one said, "Our game is done!"

So five little people all walked away.
They never even got to play.

We're Telling the Teacher on You

"We're telling the teacher on you!"
"We're telling the teacher on you!"

Wait a minute! That's not fair!
The teacher wasn't even there.

She won't know what it's about,
So let's sit down and work it out.

I Forgot to Say "Please" and "Thank You"

I forgot to say "Please" and "Thank you."
I forgot to take turns with the ball.
I forgot to say "May I?" and "Sorry."
I forgot to use manners at all.

The other kids tried to remind me,
But I just forgot what to say.
Then *they* all forgot *their* manners—
They forgot to invite me to play.

There Are Only Two Kinds of "I'm Sorry"

There are only two kinds of "I'm sorry,"
With no other kind in between.
There's the one that someone *tells* you to say,
And the one that you really mean.

You Can Use It

You can use it,
Reuse it,
Recycle it,
   and then
You can use it,
Reuse it, and
Recycle it again.

Or. . .

You can use it,
Abuse it,
Throw it on
   the ground,
Till all you see
   is trash
When you look
   around.

Or. . .

You can use it,
Reuse it,
Recycle it,
   and then
You can use it,
Reuse it, and
Recycle it again.

We Give Thanks

We give thanks
In late November.

But what about January
February
March
April
May
June
July
August
September
October
and December?

The best time for Thanksgiving
Is every day we're living.

Boring, Boring, Boring

Boring, boring, boring.
That's what my world would be
If everybody looked and talked
And acted just like me.

About the Author

Judy Lalli teaches second grade at Paul V. Fly School in Norristown, Pennsylvania, where she has taught for 26 years. She holds B.S. and M.S. degrees from the University of Pennsylvania, and she has completed extensive postgraduate work as well. As an adjunct professor for Wilkes University and Allentown College, Ms. Lalli teaches graduate education courses for teachers.

I Like Being Me is Ms. Lalli's fourth book. Her earlier books, also photographed by Douglas L. Mason-Fry, include *Feelings Alphabet*, a celebration of 26 emotions portrayed through photographs and word graphics, and *Make Someone Smile and 40 More Ways to Be a Peaceful Person*, a book on peacemaking and conflict resolution for all ages. Ms. Lalli is also the coauthor with Mary Martha Whitworth of *A Leader's Guide to I Like Being Me*.

About the Photographer

Douglas L. Mason-Fry set up his first darkroom at the age of ten and has been taking pictures ever since. He particularly enjoys the challenge of photographing children and capturing their ever-changing expressions. Mr. Mason-Fry lives in Lancaster, Pennsylvania.